Dear Year

LETTERS OF **GRATITUDE**

A Twelve-month letter journal experience

Copyright © 2023 by Lissedia Batista-Gonzalez

All rights reserved.

No portion of this book may be reproduced in any form without written permission from the publisher or author, except as permitted by U.S. copyright law.

Cover design and other illustrations by Kasia Piatek

This journal belongs to...

_____

_____

Gratitude is one of the most positive emotions we can feel. It's the ability to feel thankful for everything and everyone we have in our lives. It's our readiness to show kindness to others and, most importantly, ourselves.

In a world where life can be exhausting and has the power to leave us deflated and uninspired, gratitude is the antidote.

> "Sometimes the bad things that happen in our lives put us directly on the path to the best things that will ever happen to us."
>
> –Nicole Reed

I invite you to use this journal to focus on the now and appreciate everything around you. Write a letter of gratitude at the end of each month by focusing on the little wins, and eventually you will realize how whole your life is.

Ready.

Set.

Be grateful.

VISION BOARD (Set your intentions for the year)

Cut and paste or draw

January

"The single greatest thing you can do to change your life today would be to start being grateful for what you have right now."
— *Oprah Winfrey*

LET YOUR GRATITUDE SHINE BRIGHT

FILL THE SUN'S RAYS

January

___ / ___ / _____

January

January

January

January

January

February

"Gratitude makes sense of our past,
brings peace for today, and creates
a vision for tomorrow."
— *Melody Beattie*

A HEART BURSTING WITH GRATITUDE

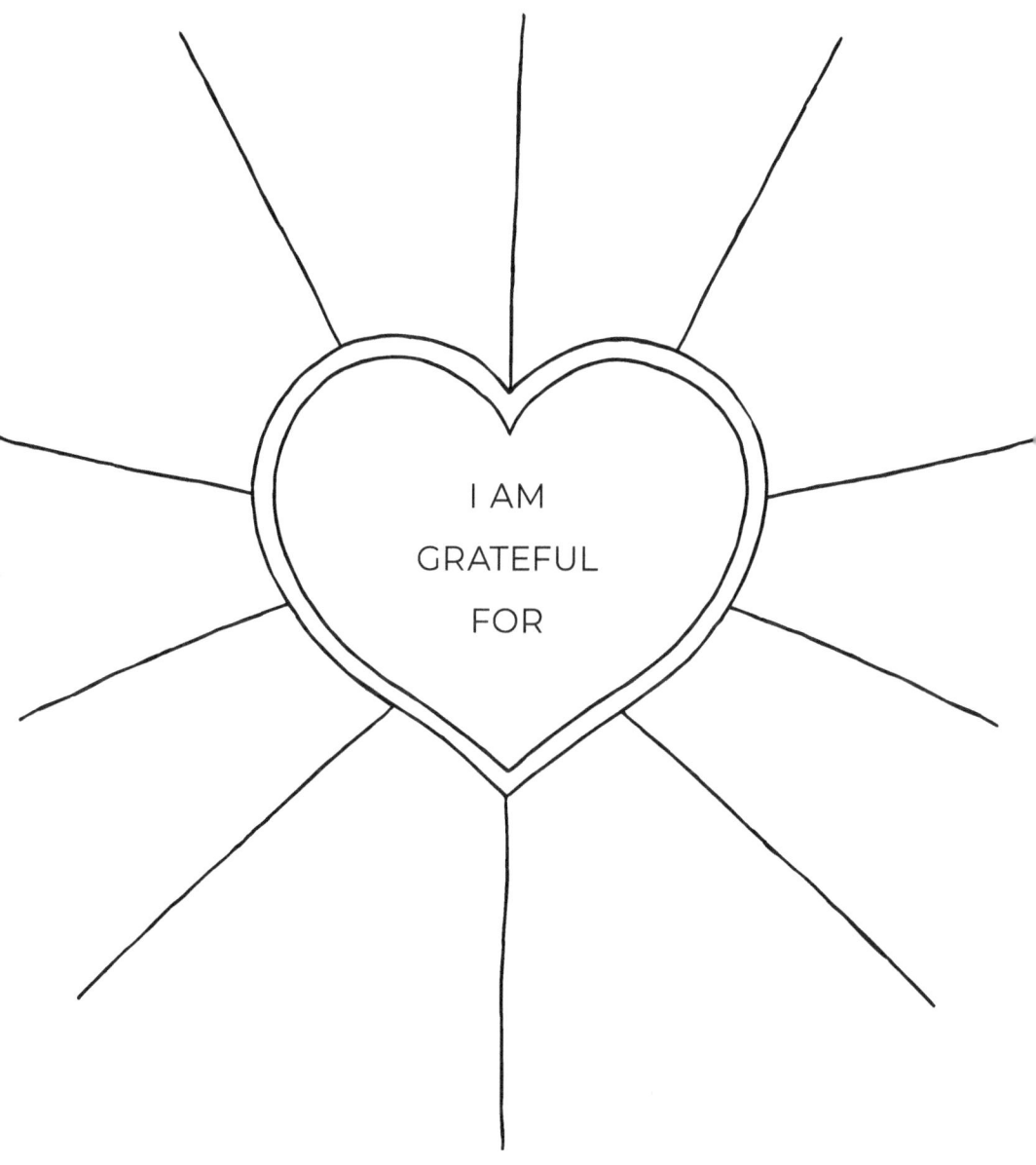

FILL THE HEART

February

___ / ___ / _____

February

February

February

February

February

March

"When gratitude becomes an essential foundation in our lives, miracles start to appear everywhere."
— *Emmanuel Dagher*

GRATITUDE HELPS ME GROW

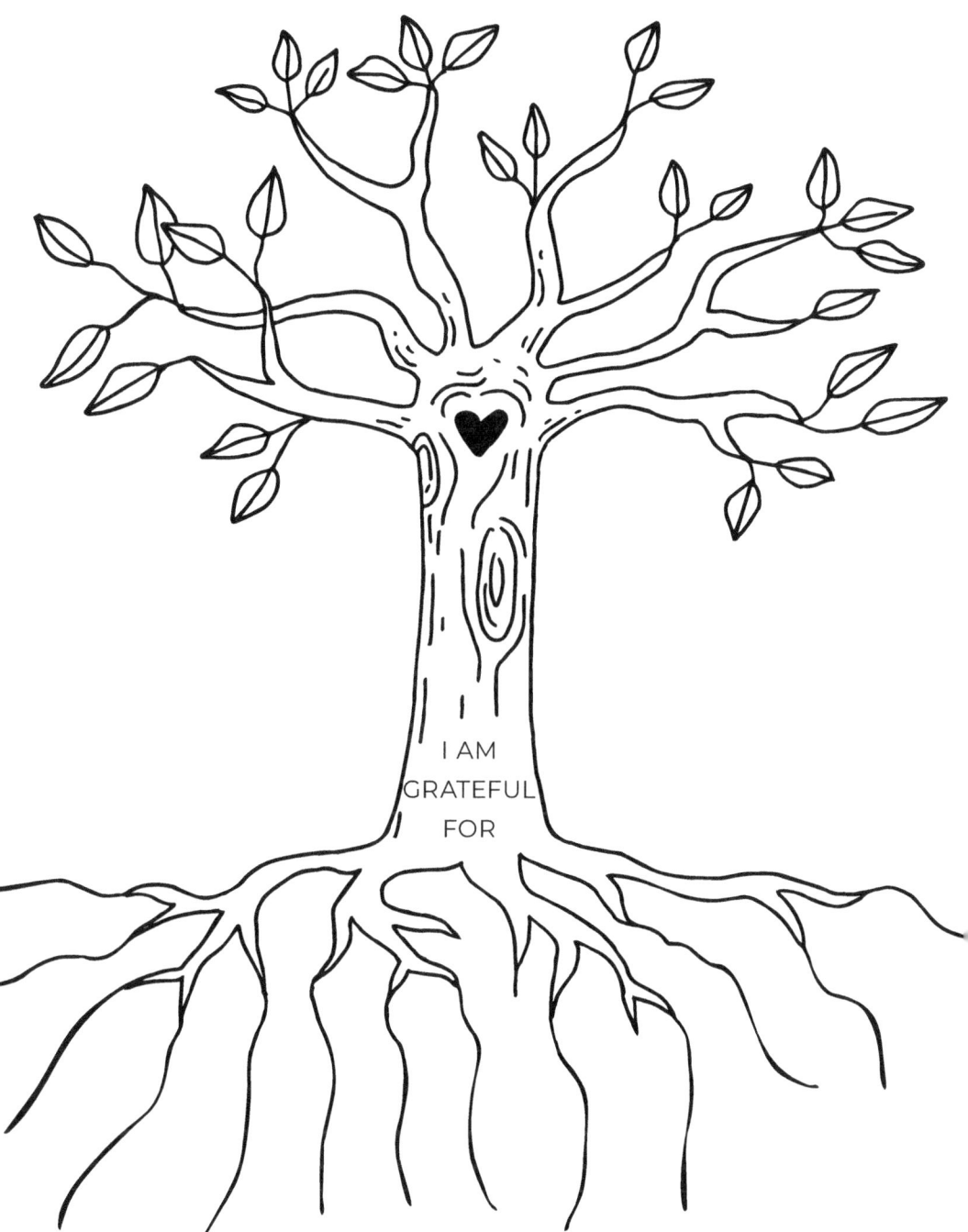

FEED THE ROOTS WITH YOUR GRATITUDE

March

___ / ___ / _____

March

March

March

March

March

April

"Gratitude is the fairest blossom
which springs from the soul."
— *Henry Ward Beecher*

A SHOWER OF GRATITUDE

FILL THE RAINDROPS

___ / ___ / _____

April

April

May

"Joy is the simplest form of gratitude."
— *Karl Barth*

GRATITUDE IS IN FULL BLOOM

I AM GRATEFUL FOR

FILL THE FLOWERS

May

___ / ___ / _____

May

May

May

May

June

"Happiness is letting go of what you think your life is supposed to look like and celebrating it for everything that it is."
— *Mandy Hale*

I AM GRATEFUL FOR A LIST OF THINGS...

I AM GRATEFUL FOR

WRITE A LIST

June

June

___ / ___ / _____

June

June

June

June

June

July

"...it is not joy that makes us grateful; it is gratitude that makes us joyful."
— *David Steindl-Rast*

TAKING NOTES OF MY GRATITUDES

FILL THE STICKY NOTES

July

July

___ / ___ / _____

July

July

July

July

July

August

"Learn to be thankful for what
you already have, while you pursue
all that you want."
— *Jim Rohn*

GRATITUDE IS A TREAT

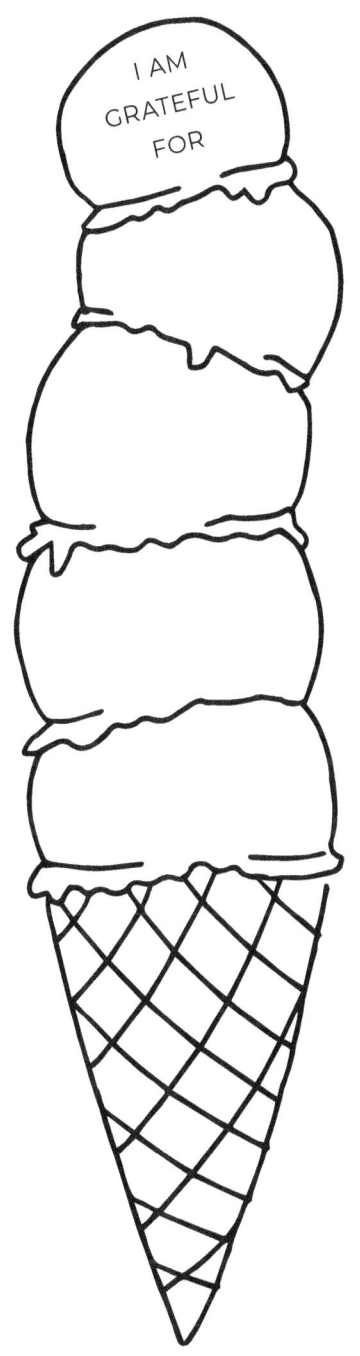

FILL THE CONE WITH SWEET GRATITUDE

August

August

___ / ___ / _____

August

August

August

August

August

September

"If you keep searching for everything beautiful in the world, you
will eventually become it."
— *Tyler Kent White*

A SWIRL OF GRATITUDE

GO AROUND WITH GRATITUDE

September

___ / ___ / _____

September

September

September

September

September

October

"This is a wonderful day,
I've never seen it before."
— *Maya Angelou*

FALL INTO A WORLD OF GRATITUDE

FILL THE LEAVES WITH GRATITUDE

October

___ / ___ / _____

October

October

October

October

October

November

"Gratitude turns what we have into enough."
— *Melody Beattie*

GRATITUDE IS A GIFT

FILL EACH BALLOON

November

___ / ___ / _____

November

November

November

November

November

December

"The real gift of gratitude is that the more grateful you are, the more present you become."
— *Robert Holden*

CELEBRATE WITH GRATITUDE

FILL THE COFFETI

December

___ / ___ / _____

December

December

December

December

VISION BOARD (Set your intentions for the next year)

Cut and paste or draw

www.ingramcontent.com/pod-product-compliance
Lightning Source LLC
Chambersburg PA
CBHW071353080526
44587CB00017B/3094